Alex, Welcome

HOUSING WEALTH CONVERSATIONS

12 SIMPLE WAYS

TO INTRODUCE THE BENEFITS OF A REVERSE MORTGAGE

HOUSING WEALTH INSTITUTE

DON GRAVES, RICP®, CLTC®, CSA
Chief Conversation Starter

P: 215-732-0814
E: Don@DonGraves.com
www.HousingWealth.net

DON GRAVES, RICP®, CLTC®, CSA

ISBN: 978-1-7320270-5-3

Book Design by HMDPUBLISHING

BONUS RESOURCES

visit www.HousingWealthConversations/bonus
for additional free resources and videos.

DISCLAIMER

The examples and case studies in the book are given for illustrative purposes only. They should not be considered tax, financial planning, or legal advice. Individuals should consult a professional regarding their specific situation.

Moreover, any calculations illustrated are hypothetical and reflective of the program rates and terms at the time of publication.

CONTENTS

ACKNOWLEDGMENTS

I want to begin by expressing gratitude to God for the guidance and inspiration throughout the creation of this book. I also extend my heartfelt thanks to my wife, Shelle, whose unwavering support and encouragement have been my anchor.

Special appreciation goes to my dedicated assistant, Emily Abbott, whose organizational skills and assistance have been invaluable in bringing this project to fruition. I am also deeply grateful to the entire team of editors, reviewers, and contributors who lent their expertise and insights, refining this book to its best possible version. Your collaborative efforts have made a significant impact, and I am truly thankful for your contributions.

INTRODUCTION

Do you find yourself struggling to introduce the benefits of reverse mortgages to your clients? Are you tired of navigating the delicate terrain of discussing this crucial aspect of retirement planning?

Despite its undeniable potential to substantially enhance retirement outcomes, many advisors hesitate to broach this topic. Fear not! This Quick Start guide is designed to empower you with the confidence and knowledge needed to initiate these crucial conversations seamlessly.

Within these pages, I delve into the 12 most common retirement income discussions advisors engage in with their clients. From strategies to minimize income taxes to preserving assets from premature erosion, I cover it all. Additionally, I lay out my Four-Step approach to introducing the reverse mortgage conversation to clients who may find this tool valuable in their overall retirement planning strategy.

Drawing from my 25 years of experience serving over 16,000 clients, this book simplifies and synthesizes the most pertinent insights advisors need. It offers straightforward solutions to address retirement concerns and kickstart new planning dialogues with both current and prospective clients.

Consider this: more than 80% of retirees own a home, representing a significant portion of their wealth—over $15 trillion in Senior Home Equity in the United States alone. Despite this wealth, retirees often grapple with fears of outliving their savings, compounded by the absence of concrete retirement plans and guidance from financial professionals. It's clear that comprehensive planning, inclusive of housing wealth, is essential.

While I emphasize the benefits of incorporating a reverse mortgage into a retirement income plan, I also recognize that it will not always be the right path for every client. It is crucial to approach this option with prudence, acknowledging it as a "potential benefit" rather than a guaranteed solution.

"Housing Wealth Conversations: 12 Simple Ways to Introduce the Benefits of a Reverse Mortgage" serves as your go-to resource, equipping you with practical tools and strategies to bridge the gap and introduce reverse mortgages effectively.

HOW BILL BELICHICK CHANGED RETIREMENT PLANNING FOREVER

In the world of sports where legends are made and legacies are forged, there exists a tale of strategy so audacious, so unconventional, that it transcends the boundaries of the game itself.

Several years back, I stumbled upon a crazy story that gripped me like no other. It's a story that captivates the imagination and challenges the very essence of what it means to compete at the highest level.

Picture this: the year is 2007, and all eyes are on the New England Patriots as they march through the NFL season with an air of invincibility. Under the masterful guidance of Coach Bill Belichick, the Patriots are a well-oiled machine, steamrolling their opponents with ruthless efficiency. Led by the iconic Tom Brady and bolstered by the electrifying talent of Randy Moss, this team is on a mission to etch their names into the annals of football history.

As the regular season unfolded, the Patriots rewrote the record books, notching win after win with an unprecedented 16-0 record. Their offense was unstoppable, shattering long-standing records and striking fear into the hearts of their adversaries. With each passing game, the aura of inevitability surrounding the Patriots grew stronger, and whispers of an undefeated season began to swirl.

But amidst the fervor and excitement, there lingered a sense of unease—a nagging doubt that threatened to undermine the Patriots' quest for greatness. Despite their dominance on the field there were whispers of skepticism, murmurs of uncertainty that cast a shadow over their seemingly inevitable march to glory.

It was in that moment of uncertainty that Coach Belichick made a decision that forever altered the course of football history. In a move that defied logic and convention, he announced a bold strategy (though not revealed to the public) for the upcoming Super Bowl—a strategy that would leave fans and pundits alike scratching their heads in disbelief.

As the Patriots took the field for the biggest game of the season, the tension was palpable. The eyes of the world were upon them, waiting to see what Coach Belichick had up his sleeve. Will it pay off, or will it unravel in spectacular fashion?

And then, as the opening kickoff approached, Coach Belichick delivered his masterstroke—a move so unexpected, so daring, that it left even the most seasoned football analysts speechless.

He deliberately started only 10 players instead of the usual 11 for the opening kickoff and then persisted with this strategy of having 10 players vs. 11 throughout the entire game—both on offense and defense!

This decision sent shockwaves through the stadium and set the stage for one of the most unforgettable moments in sports history.

As the game unfolded and the drama reached its climax, the true genius of Coach Belichick's strategy became clear. With each play, each pass, each tackle, the Patriots proved that they were more than the sum of their parts—that they were a team united in purpose and driven by a singular vision of greatness.

And when the final whistle blew and the confetti rained down from the sky, it wasn't just a victory for the Patriots—it was a triumph of innovation, a testament to the power of daring to think differently and challenge the status quo.

Remember this story?

No?

That's because it never actually happened!

No head coach in any sport, especially on the biggest stage of them all, would dare to do anything less than field their best assets because the objective is simple: position their team for the greatest chance of victory.

Just as no coach would dream of leaving out their best players in a championship game, we as financial professionals must recognize the modern reverse mortgage as the indispensable 11th player on the retirement income playing field; and as such, should not be left out of the conversation.

Today's retirement will be longer, more expensive, and less predictable than anyone imagined. It is literally the biggest game and gamble of a retiree's life, and to have anything less than the best assets on the field would be insane.

Historically, the financial services community has either dismissed the reverse mortgage or relegated it to use as a last resort. However, much has changed with the program's recent restructuring. Advisors are discovering how Housing Wealth can help their clients increase cash flow, reduce risks, preserve assets, improve liquidity, and add new investable dollars back into their savings through strategies that are appropriate, ethical, and compliant.

In the game of retirement, the stakes are high, and every tool at our disposal counts. The modern reverse mortgage, once relegated to the sidelines, has evolved into a formidable asset, capable of transforming retirement outcomes.

While it may seem unconventional to some, its importance cannot be overstated.

Just as Coach Belichick's audacious strategy in this fictitious story was ill-informed and would ultimately backfire, to overlook the modern reverse mortgage in retirement income planning is to risk missing out on a crucial tool that could significantly impact our clients' financial well-being.

So let us embark on this journey together, as we explore and perhaps write the untold sports story that revolutionized retirement planning - and uncover the hidden game-changer that will shape the future of financial services.

SECTION ONE

A QUICK REVIEW OF THE BASICS

CHAPTER 1

IT'S JUST A MORTGAGE UNDERSTANDING THE REVERSE MORTGAGE

At its core, a reverse mortgage is simply another type of mortgage, yet it uniquely caters to the financial needs of retirees. The modern reverse mortgage was established in 1988 during the seating of the 100th Congress and signed into law by our 40th President Ronald W. Reagan. The legal and most common name is the Home Equity Conversion Mortgage (HECM).

Designed for homeowners aged 62 and older, reverse mortgages allow individuals to convert part of the equity in their home into cash without the obligation to sell their home, relinquish ownership, or take on a new monthly mortgage payment.

- **What is a Reverse Mortgage?** A loan that allows you to borrow money from your home's equity without having to make mandatory mortgage payments until you move from the home or decease.
- **How much money do reverse mortgages make available?** The amount of proceeds is based on the age of the youngest spouse, the value of the home and the current interest rates.
- **What types of properties are eligible?** A generally acceptable list of properties include: 1–4-unit properties, manufactured homes that meet FHA requirements, modular homes, and some condos.

- **What are the requirements once you get the loan?** At least one borrower must live in the home as their primary residence, maintain the home in reasonable repair, keep homeowners' insurance in force, and pay property-related charges like taxes and HOA fees.
- **Are there any financial or credit requirements?** The lender will review the borrower's credit and property charge history, as well as monthly residual income, to ensure the loan offers a sustainable solution for each homeowner. It's crucial that borrowers can cover their property expenses and monthly bills both now and in the future.
- **How can the proceeds be received?** You may have the funds in a revolving line of credit with compounding growth feature, as a Lump Sum, or in fixed monthly advancements either for the duration of your time in the home or for a specific time period.
- **When is the loan repaid?** The loan is repaid when the last surviving borrower moves, dies, or sells the property.
- **What gets repaid?** The repayment amount is the combination of whatever funds have been distributed, plus any accrued interest. The reverse mortgage is a non-recourse loan, which means that neither the borrower nor their heirs will owe more than the home is worth at the time it is sold.
- **What is left to my heirs or estate?** The heirs can choose to refinance a reverse mortgage and make their own monthly payments, or simply sell the home, pay off the reverse mortgage loan balance, and have 100% of any remaining funds for themselves.
- **What are the standard closing costs on a typical Reverse Mortgage?**

The Home Equity Conversion Mortgage has (3) standard retail costs that are financed into the loan.

- Initial Mortgage Insurance Premium (IMIP): This is the United States Department of Housing and Urban Development charge for insuring the loan. It is 2% of the home's appraised value up to the HECM Limit.

- Lender Origination: The origination fee covers a lender's operating expenses associated with originating the reverse mortgage. A lender can charge the greater of $2,500 or 2% of the first $200,000 of your home's value plus 1% of the amount over $200,000. HECM origination fees are capped at $6,000.
- 3rd Party Charges: These are items such as title insurance, credit report, recording fees etc.

The client's out-of-pocket charges will include an appraisal fee and a counseling fee generally paid directly to appraisal management company and counseling agency. Currently totaling around $450.

	HOME VALUES				
STANDARD CLOSING COSTS	**$200,000**	**$400,000**	**$600,000**	**$800,000**	**$1mil**
Initial Mortgage Insurance Premium	$4,000	$8,000	$12,000	$16,000	$20,000
Lender Origination	$4,000	$6,000	$6,000	$6,000	$6,000
3rd Party Closing Costs (Varies)	$2,000	$3,000	$4,500	$6,000	$7,500

What are the Alternatives?

Most advisors would agree that the benefit derived from any financial plan, product or strategy should far outweigh any costs. The reverse mortgage is no different. If the benefits to the retirement plan outcomes and client's peace of mind are not substantially improved by incorporating the reverse mortgage, then other alternatives to meet the clients' concerns should be addressed. Here are eight alternatives:

- ☐ Sell and Move
- ☐ Borrow From Family
- ☐ Take Out or Refinance Your Existing Loan
- ☐ Use Money from Your Assets
- ☐ Take in a Roommate
- ☐ Local Program

- ☐ Go Back to Work
- ☐ Do Nothing

Remember the Four Nevers

- Never give up ownership or come off title.
- Never owe more than the home's value.
- Never have to leave the home if funds are depleted.
- Never have to make loan payments in advance of leaving the home.

www.HousingWealthConversations.com/IJAM

CHAPTER 2

THE HIDDEN FLEXIBILITY OF THE REVERSE MORTGAGE LINE OF CREDIT

Imagine if you found out your home could serve as a financial safety net, growing tax-free at a rate of 6-8%, potentially surpassing a million dollars. Would you want to know more?

Utilizing home equity is a familiar concept; many of us have leveraged it to purchase our first homes or fund renovations. But what about in retirement? What constitutes an age-appropriate equity release strategy? Monthly loan payments for decades may not align with retirees' financial goals.

Enter the **Home Equity Conversion Mortgage (HECM)** line of credit, a remarkable tool introduced in 1988. Unlike traditional home equity loans or lines of credit, the HECM line of credit allows the unused portion of reverse mortgage proceeds to grow. What's more, as long as clients meet program requirements, this line of credit cannot be frozen, canceled, capped, or reduced.

Referred to as the "Swiss Army Knife of Retirement Income Planning" in a 2015 Forbes article, the reverse mortgage boasts numerous benefits, including its **growing line of credit**.

The graphic below illustrates the initial benefit amounts for a 65-year-old at various home prices, showcasing the key feature: the unused portion of the line of credit grows over time. Suppose a 65-year-old with a $600,000 home gets a $178,800 line of credit. 10 years later, if no funds have been withdrawn and annualized growth has been between 6-8%, the line of credit would have grown to $372,975. 20 years later under the same circumstances, the line of credit would have grown to $778,021.

		HOME VALUES			
YEAR	**AGE**	**$400,000**	**$600,000**	**$800,000**	**$1,000,000**
0	65	$117,200	$178,800	$240,400	$302,000
5	70	$169,271	$258,240	$347,209	$436,177
10	75	$244,478	$372,975	$501,472	$629,969
15	80	$353,098	$538,686	$779,531	$909,861
20	85	$509,978	$778,021	$1,046,064	$1,314,107
25	90	$736,978	$1,123,692	$1,510,826	$1,897,959
30	95	$1,063,809	$1,622,944	$2,172,078	$2,741,213

In a recent Yahoo Finance article titled **"14 Key Signs You Will Run Out of Money in Retirement,"** several crucial factors were highlighted:

- Lack of a Long-Term Care Plan
- Underestimation of Life Expectancy
- Inadequate Planning for High Healthcare Costs
- Failure to Account for Inflation
- Neglecting Big-Ticket Expenses
- Alterations in Spending Habits
- Loaning Money to Children
- Spoiling Grandchildren
- Overlooking Taxes
- Disregarding Fees
- Experiencing Divorce
- Taking on Additional Debt
- Withdrawing Excessive Funds Annually
- Ignoring Market Fluctuations

What's remarkable is that 13 out of these 14 indicators can be effectively managed through the utilization of the Growing HECM Line of Credit.

When the program began in 1988, the architects believed that reverse mortgage proceeds would be used primarily in a lump sum fashion. However, about 10 or 15 years ago, new research indicated that delayed, gradual use of the line of credit can enhance investment longevity.

Increasingly, financial planners acknowledge the merit of integrating a reverse mortgage line of credit into retirement strategies. Dr. Wade Pfau, Ph.D., CFA, formerly of The American College, debunks misconceptions regarding the HECM line of credit's growth. Contrary to common belief, the line of credit grows in tandem with the loan balance, potentially accruing substantial value if left untapped.

Consider this: Would your client prefer their home equity to remain liquid or locked? Growing or stagnant? Non-cancelable or cancelable? And if accessed, would they prefer payments to be voluntary or mandatory? The HECM line of credit offers the preferable option for each consideration.

Throughout this Guidebook, you will see that the Growing Line of Credit is the foundation on which the majority of our Case Studies are built. It is uniquely designed for retirees and when used correctly, it truly is the 8th Wonder of the financial planning world.

www.HousingWealthConversations.com/LineOfCredit

SECTION TWO

IDENTIFYING AND INTRODUCING THE HOUSING WEALTH CONVERSATION

CHAPTER 3

THE MODERN PROFILE OF REVERSE MORTGAGE BORROWERS

Since joining the industry in 2000, I've observed significant changes in the typical reverse mortgage borrower profile. Today, clients are taking a more proactive approach to retirement planning; characterized by younger demographics and increased financial awareness. Financial advisors play a pivotal role in recognizing clients who could benefit from discussions about housing wealth.

Here are five common client profiles:

- **Constrained**: These clients are in dire circumstances, with no other assets or income left.
- **Concerned**: They need to rescue their retirement income due to unforeseen circumstances.
- **Cautious**: Clients have a workable retirement plan but lack contingency for unexpected expenses.
- **Comfortable**: They seek enhancements to their retirement plans despite having a decent one already.
- **Carefree**: Clients have a solid retirement plan and the financial stability to handle any shocks.

Surprisingly, there is no typical client. So, what basic criteria should an advisor consider?

Age: At least one spouse is aged 62 or older

Homeownership: Clients own a home.

Seems straightforward, right?

Through numerous conversations, I've encountered diverse client profiles and scenarios. The modern reverse mortgage empowers retirees across all economic backgrounds to achieve a more secure retirement. Understanding the varied types of borrowers allows financial advisors to tailor their approach and provide optimal solutions.

BORROWER PROFILES

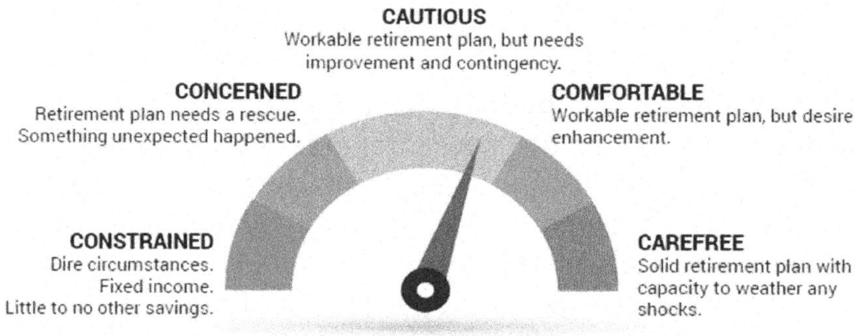

Here are a few remarkable client examples:

High Net Worth Individual: La Jolla, CA: A client with $45 million in retirement savings and a $10 million home faced a significant capital gains bill. After consultation with his attorney, accountant, and financial advisor, the reverse mortgage emerged as the most cost-effective solution.

Retired Pharmaceutical CEO: With $5 million in investments and a $4.5 million FJersey Shore home, the client sought to secure a multi-million-dollar life insurance policy without compromising financial stability. Reverse mortgages were integrated into the strategy.

Financial Emergency: A widow with a million-dollar retirement nest egg iFmpulsively withdrew $452,000 to buy her only child a home, jeopardizing her financial security. By using a reverse mortgage, we were able to restore the funds she withdrew and eliminate her need to pay taxes on those dollars.

Knowing When to Introduce Reverse Mortgages and Addressing Compliance Concerns

In every industry, there are individuals whose actions can impact everyone else. When it comes to reverse mortgages, compliance departments vary in their approach, but there are some universal rules to follow. I call these the Four No No's:

Don't Practice Law Without a License: Speaking about reverse mortgage rates, fees, or terms without the appropriate license is a violation. Leave that to my team, who are licensed professionals.

Don't Use the Direct Proceeds for Any Products: While borrowers can use the proceeds as they wish, it's generally frowned upon to use them to purchase other products directly.

Don't Receive Any Compensation: Mortgage companies cannot compensate unlicensed individuals in any form.

Don't Make a Recommendation to Buy: It's best to take an "Education Only" position rather than recommending a reverse mortgage outright. Trust professionals like my team to provide guidance in this area.

When is the Best Time to Broach the Subject Matter?

Housing Wealth via the Modern Reverse Mortgage is a valuable tool, representing a significant portion of many retirees' wealth. Not discussing it would be akin to playing the Super Bowl with only 10 players.

Bring up the topic at client review meetings, when discussing retirement concerns, or whenever the conversation naturally leads to financial planning. My team and I are here to support you every step of the way.

www.HousingWealthConversations.com/Profiles

CHAPTER 4

35 WAYS CLIENTS ARE ALREADY INQUIRING ABOUT REVERSE MORTGAGES

"My clients have never asked me about a reverse mortgage."

This is something I have frequently heard from my financial advisor partners over the years. While this assertion holds weight initially, often a deeper examination reveals a more nuanced reality. Despite not explicitly mentioning "reverse mortgages," clients often indirectly express interest or curiosity about them through their inquiries and concerns.

But how?

Consider this analogy: Every year, hardware and home improvement stores sell millions of power drills worldwide. Curiously, few purchasers specifically seek out a drill per se; rather, they seek the means to create a hole. The drill becomes a means to an end, a solution to their problem or fulfillment of their goal.

Similarly, your clients may not articulate a desire for a reverse mortgage, but they're undoubtedly expressing interest in the financial solutions it provides.

They're asking for the "hole," not the "drill." Herein lies the challenge: decoding the various ways in which clients indirectly inquire about the suitability of a reverse mortgage, and then helping them access the resources to make an informed decision.

Outlined below are 35 subtle inquiries that your clients have likely made regarding the ideal tool to achieve their financial objectives. Can you identify a few that you have heard?

- ☐ Will we have sufficient income to enjoy our retirement after we fully retire?
- ☐ Will the money we have now last as long as we need it?
- ☐ What is our plan if we prematurely run out of savings?
- ☐ Can we do anything to manage the external forces that can prematurely erode our savings?
- ☐ Should we maintain a Home Equity Line of Credit for emergencies or expenses?
- ☐ What is our plan if inflation goes up again in the future?
- ☐ Are we prepared for health and long-term care costs?
- ☐ Can we create a plan to lower or manage the taxes we are paying or could be paying in retirement?
- ☐ How can I keep more of my money invested for earnings and stay in the lowest tax bracket?
- ☐ Can I enjoy my retirement savings and still leave a considerable inheritance?
- ☐ How will we replace social security when one of us passes?
- ☐ Should I keep my mortgage or pay it off with my savings?
- ☐ Are we able to move to a more expensive home?
- ☐ How can I liquidate assets to donate to charity without disrupting my retirement goals?
- ☐ How do I finance a new home after retirement or the passing of a spouse?
- ☐ How do I best support my children and grandchildren without compromising my retirement savings?

- ☐ What do I do when Long-Term Care Insurance premiums rise significantly when needed most?
- ☐ How can I defer my social security when I need income today?
- ☐ How can I replace the income I was getting from my deceased spouse's SS check?
- ☐ Can I reduce my provisional income, so my social security is not taxed?
- ☐ Is there a way for me to pay less in Medicare IRMAA Surcharge?
- ☐ Can we limit our withdrawals to the required minimum distributions only? What if we need more than that?
- ☐ How would I financially navigate in the event of a divorce?
- ☐ How do I finance home maintenance needs and modernization without depleting my retirement savings?
- ☐ How can I plan retirement while keeping up with all my expenses? (HOA fees, Property Taxes, Utilities, Insurance, Mortgage)?
- ☐ How do I manage retirement planning with the ongoing expenses of owning a home?
- ☐ What is the best way for me to manage my mortgage during retirement?
- ☐ What if I need to draw more than I usually do when my stocks are losing value?
- ☐ Can I increase my spending from my portfolio without jeopardizing my nest egg?
- ☐ Can I trim expenses from investments while still enjoying early retirement years?
- ☐ What if household income decreases due to market performance or unexpected expenses?
- ☐ Can I buy a second home near family without jeopardizing our retirement plans?

- ☐ How can we cover monthly expenses and avoid selling assets at depressed values?
- ☐ How can we fill the gap in a retirement plan caused by lower-than-expected returns?
- ☐ How would I pay for short-term in-home care or physical therapy following an accident or medical episode?

Have you heard any of those sentiments in your practice?

Of course you have! Every time you hear them, your client is asking for a hole and now you can tell them about a drill they may not have considered.

www.HousingWealthConversations.com/35Ways

CHAPTER 5

MASTERING CLIENT CONVERSATIONS THE FOUR STEPS

Despite the potential of reverse mortgages to significantly improve retirement outcomes for clients, many advisors shy away from broaching the subject due to the negative connotations and unfavorable media coverage associated with these financial instruments. Instead of addressing the topic head-on, some advisors opt to avoid it altogether.

However, with a structured approach grounded in empathy and understanding, financial advisors can skillfully introduce the concept of reverse mortgages to their clients in a manner that is both respectful and empowering.

In this chapter, we'll explore the **Four Steps**, a straightforward approach to introducing reverse mortgages to clients whom you believe will find this tool valuable in their overall retirement planning strategy.

STEP ONE: OBTAIN PERMISSION

Although reverse mortgages offer numerous benefits, they often carry misconceptions and stigmas, presenting a challenge when introducing them to clients.

One effective strategy to overcome this challenge is by obtaining your client's permission to discuss the topic within the context of their overall retirement plan. By framing the conversation around housing wealth as an integral part of a holistic approach to retirement income, you can seamlessly integrate reverse mortgages as one of the potential solutions for securing a comfortable retirement.

This approach establishes a foundation for productive dialogue and helps alleviate any apprehensions your clients may have about exploring unfamiliar financial options.

Introducing the Fourth Bucket Strategy for Asset Diversification

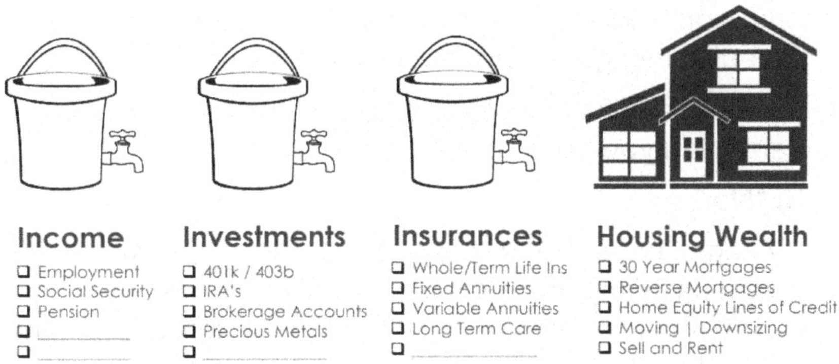

In the chart above, you can see the four primary buckets that most retirees have access to. Interestingly, 87% of them possess the fourth bucket, yet they are often unsure how or where it could contribute to their retirement.

As we progress, we'll delve into several concepts related to these buckets. But for now, let me introduce you to a straightforward yet impactful dialogue that incorporates the 'Four Buckets.'

The AAA Permission Dialogue

Advisor: "Mr. and Mrs., as we are crafting your retirement income strategy, do you believe it's important to consider all available assets?"

Client: "Yes, we do."

Advisor: "What I'm referring to is the fact that most retirees have access to four significant asset categories:

- Income Bucket: comprising Social Security, pensions, employment income, etc.
- Investment Bucket: encompassing IRAs, 401(k)s, brokerage accounts, etc.
- Insurance Bucket: involving fixed and variable annuities, whole and term life insurance, long-term care insurance, etc.
- Housing Wealth Bucket: involving 30-year mortgages, home equity loans, reverse mortgages, home equity lines of credit, selling, renting, downsizing, etc."

Advisor: "Thus, when designing your retirement strategy, is there anything you believe should be excluded?"

Client: "No."

Many clients have been exposed to negative narratives about various financial tools such as whole life insurance, annuities, the stock market, reverse mortgages, or determining a sustainable withdrawal rate. It's possible that we may not fully understand their preconceptions.

The essence of this dialogue lies in framing not only reverse mortgages but all these strategies within the context of building a successful retirement income plan. It prompts the essential question: "Should anything be excluded as we develop your plan?"

Typically, the most rational response at this juncture is "No," indicating that nothing should be disregarded as we proceed.

There you have it! You've effectively obtained permission to discuss reverse mortgages by positioning them alongside other legitimate tools for retirement income planning.

STEP TWO: DISCOVER THE PRESSURE POINTS

Growing up in Kentucky, I learned a lot from old tales spun around the porch. Here's one that always stuck with me:

The Paperboy

As a young paperboy made his rounds through the Kentucky countryside, he stumbled upon an old farmer sitting on his porch, his faithful dog by his side. The boy couldn't help but notice the dog's distressed whimpering, a clear sign that something was off.

"Sir, what's wrong with your dog?" the boy asked, concern evident in his voice.

With a weathered sigh, the farmer replied, "Oh, he laid on a nail."

Perplexed, the boy asked, "Then why don't he move?"

The farmer leaned back in his rocking chair and offered a sage explanation, "Well, son, it just don't hurt him enough to move."

Ready to Make a Change?

This story teaches us a valuable lesson about human behavior and financial decision-making. Much like the farmer's dog, there are individuals who endure financial discomfort without taking any proactive steps to address their situation. Despite feeling the weight of their financial worries, they often remain stagnant, unwilling to explore new paths or embrace change until the pressure becomes too overwhelming to bear.

Understanding the potential significance of reverse mortgages in your clients' financial journeys requires a deep dive into their specific concerns, challenges, and aspirations. It necessitates attentive listening to their needs and uncovering the pain points they encounter in retirement planning.

Whether it's the looming fear of financial insufficiency, the burden of escalating healthcare expenses, or the desire to sustain their desired lifestyle in retirement, identifying these concerns provides invaluable insight into how reverse mortgages can seamlessly integrate into their unique circumstances.

However, it's not merely about discovering the points of financial pressure or pain for your clients; it's equally crucial to assess whether these concerns hold enough weight for them to contemplate making a change. Only then can we initiate discussions about leveraging housing wealth as a potential solution.

If clients are not yet ready to take action, it's prudent to refrain from introducing the topic prematurely. Just as the farmer's dog needed the discomfort of the nail to motivate movement, sometimes it takes a heightened sense of financial discomfort to catalyze meaningful change.

Below are five questions I use to help clients self-identify their pressure points.

Five Questions to Help Uncover Pressure Points

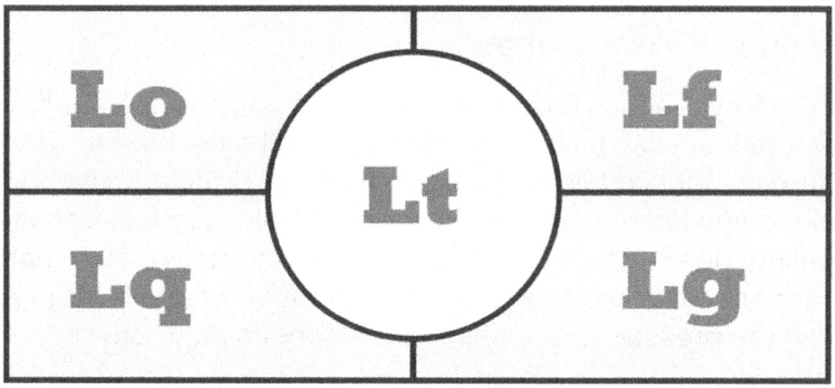

- **Longevity:** *"Will I have enough savings to meet my basic living expenses?"*

  On a scale from 1-10, how much does the thought of running out of savings trouble you?

- **Lifestyle:** *"Will I have enough money to enjoy retirement on my terms?"*

  On a scale from 1-10, how disappointed would you be if you had to adjust your standard of living to make your savings last?

- **Legacy:** *"How will I be financially remembered?"*

  On a scale from 1-10, how important is it for you to cut back on your retirement lifestyle if it meant leaving legacy for your heirs and not having to rely on them financially or otherwise?

- **Liquidity:** *"Will I have access to untaxed cash when I need it?"*

  On a scale from 1-10, how prepared are you for unexpected spending shocks in retirement?

- **Long Term Care**: *"Am I financially prepared for the costs of health-related expenses?"*

  On a scale from 1-10, how prepared would you be if you had to access an additional $300,000 for healthcare related costs?

By giving your clients a clear explanation and a range to choose from, you open up the dialogue and allow them to share each pressure point.

I think you will find it very effective.

STEP THREE: DISCUSS THE POSSIBILITIES

Over the past quarter-century, I've had the privilege of engaging with over 16,000 consumers, with nearly 3,000 of them choosing to proceed with a reverse mortgage and becoming my clients. This experience highlights two crucial points: firstly, I've had extensive discussions with a diverse range of individuals, and secondly, it underscores that a reverse mortgage isn't always the optimal solution for everyone's financial objectives.

As we look at step three of the process, "Discuss the Possibilities," it's imperative to keep in mind that initiating the conversation about housing wealth is paramount. However, it's equally essential to recognize that suitability varies from person to person.

Now that we've thoroughly understood your needs and concerns, and assessed your readiness for change, it's time to explore how reverse mortgages can fit into your broader retirement plan. To illustrate, let's consider the case of Fred and Wilma Flintstone.

CLIENT PROFILE

Fred and Wilma find themselves at a crossroads as they contemplate retirement amidst uncertainties about their desired lifestyle. Fred's back issues are complicating his work at the Quarry, adding to their financial concerns.

They currently own a $600,000 home with a $100,000 mortgage that they slowly pay down with monthly payments of $1,000. With their combined savings amount of $400,000, they simply don't know if this is enough to have the retirement they envisioned. They are eager for a change, and open to exploring various solutions.

Here is where we position the possibilities as there are several options available to address their dilemma:

- They can extend their working years to boost savings.
- They can adjust retirement expectations to align with reduced income.
- They can explore downsizing or moving in with their daughter, Pebbles, who has a spare room.

However, none of these options spark enthusiasm in Fred and Wilma's minds, leaving them in search of a solution that offers both financial stability and peace of mind in retirement.

SEVEN MAGIC WORDS: "IF YOU COULD USE YOUR HOME TO..."

Unlocking the discussion about reverse mortgages begins with this simple question - or certain variations of it.

This phrase holds the key to starting the conversation about the potential benefits of a reverse mortgage. Once you've identified the pain points, it's time to introduce the concept alongside other possibilities.

Throughout this guide, variations of these **Seven Magic Words** will emerge, but their purpose remains constant: to prompt deeper exploration.

So, let's see where the Seven Magic Words Dialogue (*"If you could use your home to..."*) comes into play with the Flintstones.

"Fred and Wilma, I'm curious, if we could use your home to eliminate the mortgage payments and create a reserve fund, would you want to see how it works?"

Let me give you a few more to try on for size:

- If you could use your home to increase your cash flow in retirement
- If you could use your home to reduce certain retirement risks
- If you could use your home to preserve your existing assets
- If you could use your home to preserve more liquidity in case of an unexpected need
- If you could use your home to create a backup plan for market risk and volatility
- If you could use your home to turn your current mortgage payment into a voluntary one
- If you could use your home to defer social security for large payouts later
- If you could use your home to supplement income during a crisis
- If you could use your home to keep your IRA's and annuities working longer
- If you could use your home to hedge against inflation

"If you could use your home to (fill in the blank), would you want to see how it works?" **or** "What would that mean to you?" You can choose either.

We are describing the benefits of the reverse mortgage as a possible solution to wherever the pressure or concern is in our client's retirement outlook.

Clients will naturally ask some questions. Here are some common responses advisors give.

When the Client Asks, "How Are You Going to Do It?"

Tell them you are going to explore a government insured home equity loan program that allows them to borrow money without having to make any mandatory monthly repayments.

When They Ask, "Is This a Reverse Mortgage?"

Tell them honestly, yes, it is, "a type of reverse mortgage". Or yes, "the newly restructured reverse mortgage" or "modern reverse mortgage" or "new reverse mortgage". But always describe it – don't just say "reverse mortgage"!

When They Ask You, "What's Different About It?"

Clients will often ask "what's different?" or they say they heard these things are bad, or expensive, or they knew someone who knew someone who knew some that got a reverse mortgage and had a bad experience!

They may ask "So, what's new about it?" When this happens, I want you to say the three hardest words for many of my advisor partners. **"I don't know!"**

That's because the program started in America in 1961, when Nelson Haynes of Deering Savings & Loan originated America's first-ever reverse mortgage in Portland, Maine. He created this unique type of loan because Nellie Young (the widowed wife of his high school football coach) didn't know how to stay in her home after losing her husband. Later, in 1988, the reverse mortgage came under the US Dept of Housing. It went through modifications and modernizations in 2013 and 2017 and gets tinkered with every October for improvement.

So, the truth is that you don't know (nor should you) all that's new or restructured.

But **what you do know** is that it can eliminate a monthly mortgage payment to allow Fred and Wilma to retire earlier and without worry. **What you do know** is that it can help create cash flow in retirement. **What you do know** is that it can help provide income during down markets so that your clients' assets are not prematurely eroded... and so on.

Emphasize that while reverse mortgages are not a "one-size-fits-all" solution, they should not be dismissed outright and deserve careful consideration alongside other financial tools.

So, ask them again.

"If we could use your home to (fill in the blank), would you want to see how it works?"

If they say no, move on, but most will say, "Yes, I would like to see how it works."

That's when you move on to our final phase. Pass the Baton!

STEP FOUR: PASS THE BATON TO YOUR TRUSTED REVERSE MORTGAGE PROFESSIONAL

While you aim to provide the best guidance, acknowledging the complexity of reverse mortgage products is key. Therefore, partnering with a trusted reverse mortgage professional (like me!) ensures that clients receive tailored advice.

This collaboration reinforces your commitment to their best interests and provides access to comprehensive support. By embracing this partnership, you offer holistic retirement solutions that include the housing wealth asset.

Together, we will navigate retirement planning with confidence, empowering clients to make informed decisions for their financial security.

Partners In Planning | Shaping the Reverse Mortgage Experience

I've crafted this guide specifically for advisors and partners who are already familiar with my work in the realm of reverse mortgages.

Understanding my role in the process is key to ensuring successful collaboration and positive client outcomes. Allow me to outline afresh the three primary things I do:

> **Education:** Throughout my nearly 25 years of experience, I've had the privilege of educating over 30,000 financial advisors. This includes creating content for courses at the American College of Financial Services and writing educational materials. I also regularly host webinars, workshops, and stage events to share knowledge.
>
> **Case Design | Consultation:** Advisors and clients rely on me to help them grasp the complexities of reverse mortgages and design strategies tailored to their retirement income goals.
>
> **Origination:** I lead a dedicated team across 49 states and oversee the entire reverse mortgage journey for our clients, ensuring a seamless process from start to finish.

I understand the critical role that the right reverse mortgage partner plays in an advisor's practice. Collaborating with a skilled and knowledgeable team is essential for achieving positive outcomes, while working with the wrong individuals can harm an advisor's reputation.

Over the years, I've built strong relationships with partners who can attest to the quality of service provided by my team. Advisors can trust that they're in capable hands when partnering with us. Effective collaboration ensures smooth execution and favorable results in the realm of reverse mortgages.

Benefits of Selecting the Right Guide:

Just as Yoda led Luke Skywalker and Gandalf led Frodo, having the right guide is essential to retirement planning. Gandalf, while being an expert guide for Frodo in returning the Ring to Mordor, wouldn't have the specialized knowledge about how to teach Luke Skywalker how to hone his use of the Force.

Even though each of these guides is extremely powerful, they are specialists in their own stories.

There are lenders out there who say, "I can do that too!" about reverse mortgages – which can be great for some consumers! However, since a financial advisor is in a high-trust position with their client, it's critically important that the people they have supporting their practice are expertly skilled and **singularly focused**. We <u>only</u> do reverse mortgages.

The reverse mortgage, though simple (It's Just a Mortgage!), requires a **skillful hand** in structuring it to align with the advisor's recommendations and helping create sustainable outcomes.

Here are a couple of real-life examples that prove that choosing the wrong partner can be harmful for your practice and a client's retirement:

- An advisor, upon doing an annual review for his client, discovered that the client had deposited an excess of $100k into her own bank account from the proceeds of a reverse mortgage. The advisor called us because he was under the impression that his client was establishing a line of credit. Why would the lender encourage her to take out a lump sum of money?

  I explained to the advisor that most reverse mortgage lenders are directly compensated based off the upfront money a client takes out. This is a conflict of interest.

Our team is **"product agnostic".** This means the compensation received is not based on how much the client takes out upfront – therefore, we can give unbiased counsel and focus on what is best for the client.

- Another lender suggested that their client take out monthly payments for a fixed amount of time. We received a call that the client was still alive and the proceeds from the reverse mortgage had run out. This strategy was ill-advised and not complementary to the plan their advisor had crafted.

Neither of these were our clients, but the advisors have since become our partners. They have discovered how treating the reverse mortgage in an isolated fashion versus incorporating it with the client's retirement plan could bring harm.

This is why you wouldn't want Gandalf to train Luke Skywalker!

We receive 95% of all our business from advisors. I have educated over 30,000 advisors about Housing Wealth during my tenure at the American College of Financial Services, and I have served over 3,000 clients. With my 25 years of **specialized experience**, you can call me the "Reverse Mortgage Yoda"!

Essential Tools for Incorporating Reverse Mortgages into Retirement Planning

As we conclude this chapter, let's focus on practical application, highlighting three essential tools that aid advisors in translating book knowledge into real-world practice: the **Customized Housing Wealth Illustration**, **Client-Facing Training**, and **Advanced Advisor Training**.

These resources are meticulously crafted from extensive field experience and direct client interactions, designed to support you in advising clients on reverse mortgages.

Customized Housing Wealth Illustration

This tool empowers advisors to generate straightforward reverse mortgage scenarios with ease. It provides clear illustrations of potential loan amounts and future credit line growth. Fundamental to the 12 discussions we delve into, it acts as a critical foundation. Despite its simplicity, it's an essential asset for advisors, streamlining the process of explaining complex financial concepts. To utilize this indispensable resource and enhance your advisory capabilities, request an illustration at www.housingwealthpro.com

Client-Facing Training

We offer a suite of educational materials including a Masterclass video series, articles, and books to help clients grasp reverse mortgage fundamentals. These resources:

- Make complex topics accessible via our Masterclass video series.
- Provide a broad spectrum of insights through articles.
- Offer in-depth understanding with comprehensive books.

They equip clients to engage in informed discussions with their advisors, ensuring they comprehend the strategic value of reverse mortgages.

Advanced Advisor Training

For advisors eager to deepen their expertise, our advanced training includes personalized coaching, webinars, and case study masterminds. This multifaceted approach ensures you stay abreast of the latest trends, regulatory changes, and innovative strategies in the reverse mortgage arena.

These tools collectively support advisors in enhancing their practice and client relationships. They reflect a commitment to empowering advisors with the knowledge and resources necessary for guiding clients toward secure retirement outcomes through the strategic use of reverse mortgages.

Next Steps for Handling a Client or Case:

- Visit www.HousingWealthPro.com to request a Housing Wealth Illustration, which will provide an estimate of your client's potential benefits from a reverse mortgage.
- Get in touch via email at AskDonGraves@gmail.com
- Set up a consultation at www.AskDonGraves.net
- Alternatively, you can reach us directly by calling 215-732-0814

What Others Are Saying

"Financial advisors who want to grow their business need to know how to help clients leverage their untapped wealth. Don's latest guide shows you how. Just like his previous works, I found this guide advisor-friendly, practical and a very usable resource. He continues to make the case for tapping into an underperforming asset and the difference reverse mortgages can possibly make in creating retirement security"

ED SLOTT, CPA | *Author and founder of www.irahelp.com Founder of Ed Slott's Elite IRA Advisor Group℠*

"I have had the pleasure of working with Don Graves at the American College, and his ability to simplify the complexities of reverse mortgages is exceptional. His extensive knowledge, practical experience and communication style make his training an immense value to any group. In fact, Don was the one who helped me get started in my exploration of reverse mortgages as a retirement income planning tool. Since then, I've written extensively on the topic. I would highly recommend Don as a resource for your next event."

WADE PFAU, PHD, CFA | *Former Professor of Retirement Income and RICP® Program Director at The American College* | *Founder of RetirementResearcher.com*

"I was skeptical of reverse mortgages...but, what Don writes about in this book shows you things [about them] you had no idea were even available. When you combine housing wealth with other retirement assets, a whole new dimension is added to what can be accomplished."

TOM HEGNA, CLU, CHFC, CASL | *Economist, Speaker, and Best-Selling Author*

"Don's expertise in the area of HECM education set the bar in the RICP program at the American College as well as within our very own industry walls. His knack to completely flip the connotation of the reverse mortgage and communicate complex strategies with ease and enthusiasm during his training workshops is a specific strength of his I admire greatly."

DR. ROBERT "BOB" JOHNSON, CFA®, CAIA® | Past President, The American College of Financial Services

"In America, and more specifically maybe within your own office and/or client list, the perception of reverse mortgages can be intensely negative. I would be the first to admit my own perception was initially skeptical. After working with

Don Graves at the American College, my opinion was turned upside down. Through powerful words and simplified language, Don will transform your perception and provide impactful strategies to ensure your retirement income needs are met. I look forward to seeing Don coach and train more people because everyone needs to hear his message today."

JAMIE HOPKINS ESQ., LLM, CFP®, CHFC®, CLU®, RICP® I CEO an Senior VP of Private Wealth at Bryn Mawn Trust I Former Director of the American College's Retirement Income Center

"The thought leaders have spoken, and I concur, when you utilize reverse mortgages, you increase the likelihood of a positive outcome in retirement."

DAVID MCKNIGHT I *Best-Selling Author, Power of Zero: The Tax Train is Coming*

"Don opened my eyes to a stream of tax-free wealth for individuals in diverse categories - from the affluent to those whose home equity represents the majority of their wealth. I have read Don's other books on the subject and have adopted what I learned from him about using a HECM into my consulting practice."

HEATHER SCHREIBER, RICP, NSSA I *Founder and President of HLS Retirement Consulting, LLC*

"Don Graves is one of the foremost experts regarding HECM regulations and reverse mortgages. When I first met him, I realized I had a bias regarding this topic and was blown away by what I did not know. I have now developed HECM strategies in our retirement planning software tool (Retirement NextGen) and have incorporated this element of training in our two-day class. Don made me a believer out of me. Every thoughtful, caring, and thorough financial professional should take the time to read his book.

CURTIS CLOKE CLTC, LUTCF, RICP I *President; Accuity Wealth and Thrive Income Systems, Adjunct Instructor, The American College RICP*

"Like many in the financial service world I was very skeptical of reverse mortgages. Don Graves helped me over that skepticism. The average American is living longer subjecting him/her to the corrosive impact of the loss of purchasing power. Tax favored access to home equity can help to offset that risk and help aging Americans in many other ways.

JOE JORDAN | *International Speaker, Recipient of 2023 John Newton Russel Memorial Award for outstanding services in life insurance, Behavioral Finance Expert*

"The reverse mortgage is widely misunderstood and underutilized. You are not a true holistic financial planner if you ignore housing wealth. Strategic use of a modern Reverse Mortgage as part of a comprehensive plan can reduce taxes, reduce risk, increase Social Security benefits, and will result in more overall retirement income. It is a game changer for an enhanced retirement while leaving a greater legacy for the family. Don is a true leader and expert in his field. He is a teacher of teachers and a pioneer in housing wealth strategies."

LANE MARTINSEN, RICP, CLTC | *President of Martinsen Wealth Management*

"This has been an important part of a solution for clients who have significant equity, would like to stay in their homes but need access to that equity capital to do so. Don is a patient instructor who educates himself on each client's financial situation and is able to portray the value of a reverse mortgage if it applies."

PHILIP MEESE | *Investment Advisor*

"Developing multiple income streams in retirement, which includes using a reverse mortgage, is essential to manage the ever-changing economy. Due to all the income pressures that retirees are dealing with today, it is essential that the reverse mortgage conversation be part of the equation. Don has been a tremendous resource for our firm, Macro Wealth

Management, and it is great knowing that we have one of the foremost authorities on this topic on our team! Another great aspect of collaborating with Don is that he breaks down the benefits of a reverse mortgage into understandable language for the client."

MART MCCLELLAN | *President of Macro Wealth Management*

"For many clients, their house is one of their most valuable assets, and yet it isn't typically even considered as part of the financial equation. Bringing housing wealth into the conversation via a reverse mortgage frees up a lot of liquidity and reduces the overall risk level for those who qualify. Don has been helpful in educating me and my clients on the potential benefits and drawbacks of a reverse mortgage, where it might fit into the equation, and how housing wealth can and should be part of a comprehensive financial plan."

LOGAN HERTZ | *Strategic Planning Group*

"I can say that having the ability to begin the Reverse Mortgage conversation with clients and prospects adds another valuable arrow into my quiver of services I can offer those individuals and families. There is never one solution available to families that will address all of their needs, wants and goals. With the Reverse Mortgage option available, I can provide more opportunities to solve any financial concerns and add excellent alternatives to the otherwise limited equity discussions. Having Don Graves available to advise me on the pros and cons of Reverse Mortgages is invaluable. Don brings 25 years of experience in the market. He has seen the good, bad and ugly of the Reverse Mortgage development and shares those insights with me in my practice and clients I introduce to the concept. Time well spent."

JERRY SHERIDAN | *LIFT-Up Financial Services*

Conclusion:

Introducing the concept of reverse mortgages to your clients doesn't have to be a daunting task. By following the approach outlined in this chapter, you can navigate the conversation with confidence, empathy, and professionalism.

Remember to obtain permission, discover the pain, discuss the possibilities, and pass the baton to your trusted reverse mortgage professional.

Together, we can empower our clients to make informed decisions that enhance their financial well-being and retirement security.

SECTION THREE

12 REVERSE MORTGAGE CONVERSATIONS

CONVERSATION #1

ENDING MANDATORY MONTHLY MORTGAGE PAYMENTS IN RETIREMENT

Question: What could retirement look like if you didn't have to make a monthly payment?

Imagine retirement without the burden of monthly mortgage payments. For many retirees, this dream seems unattainable, as a significant portion carry some form of housing debt well into their golden years. This obligation can cast a shadow over the joy of retirement, with payments stretching decades into the future.

However, eliminating a monthly mortgage through a reverse mortgage opens doors to numerous planning opportunities.

For most people in retirement, carrying some sort of monthly house payment is the norm. By some accounts up to 68% or more of baby boomers have a mortgage, second mortgage, home equity loan or home equity line of credit. At least one of them.

For some, this may not be a financial challenge; but for others, the joy of retirement is often overshadowed by the looming obligation of monthly mortgage payments, a commitment that could stretch decades.

Eliminating a monthly mortgage through a reverse mortgage unlocks multiple planning opportunities with the liberated mortgage payment proceeds it creates. Let's explore a client scenario to illustrate the transformative impact:

CLIENT PROFILE

- 65-year-old Homer and Marge are nearing retirement
- Total retirement savings in qualified plans: $650,000
- Desired initial withdrawal: $45,000 | Advisor's recommendation: $26,000
- Home valued at $650,000 with a $200,000 mortgage | Monthly principal and interest payments: $1,800.

CONCERNS, RISKS, GAPS AND OPPORTUNITIES

Homer and Marge fear that financial worries may overshadow their retirement dreams. They seek a balance between enjoying life and securing their future. The advisor shares concerns about overspending in the early retirement years, potential market volatility, and the impact of unplanned expenses on the client's nest egg.

Question: If you could eliminate your monthly mortgage payments so that you could enjoy more of your retirement early and without spending guilt, what could that mean to you?

REVERSE MORTGAGE HIGHLIGHTS

- Sufficient proceeds from the reverse mortgage to pay off the $200,000 loan balance.
- Liberation of $1,800 per month in after-tax cash flow from mortgage payments, assuming Homer and Marge take the standard deduction (very likely) and get no tax benefit from their mortgage interest payments.
- Generation of nearly $2,200 per month in pre-tax dollars.
- Reduction of initial withdrawal rate from $45,000 to $15,000, aligning with both client and advisor objectives.
- Reduction of provisional income by almost $30,000 per year, mitigating income tax liability, potential social security taxation, and IRMAA concerns.

The advent of reverse mortgages has redefined the landscape of retirement planning, offering older homeowners a path to financial autonomy and peace of mind. By eliminating mandatory mortgage payments, retirees gain the freedom to navigate their golden years with greater assurance and flexibility. This innovative approach not only alleviates financial burdens, but also enriches the retirement experience, allowing individuals to focus on what truly matters: enjoying their time to the fullest.

www.HousingWealthConversations.com/VoluntaryPayments

CONVERSATION #2

MAKING VOLUNTARY MONTHLY MORTGAGE PAYMENTS | AN UNKNOWN STRATEGY

Question: If you had a choice, would you rather your monthly mortgage payments be mandatory or voluntary, which one would you choose?

Imagine having the flexibility to choose whether your monthly mortgage payments are mandatory or voluntary. With a reverse mortgage, this becomes a reality, offering homeowners a newfound sense of control over their financial future.

CLIENT PROFILE:

- 65-year-old Clark and Lois are aiming for full retirement in their mid-70s
- Total retirement savings: $450,000
- Home valued at $650,000 with a $150,000 mortgage | Monthly principal and interest payments: $1,500.

CONCERNS, RISKS, GAPS, AND OPPORTUNITIES:

Clark and Lois worry about their retirement readiness amidst unexpected expenses and financial setbacks. They value continued work, but also desire a secure retirement. The advisor shares concerns about potential early retirement and the need for a contingency plan. Just like everyone else, Superman must hang up his cape eventually.

REVERSE MORTGAGE HIGHLIGHTS:

- Sufficient proceeds from the reverse mortgage to pay off the $150,000 loan balance, leaving a $66,000 growing reverse mortgage line of credit.
- Choice to make voluntary monthly reverse mortgage payments of $2,000 to accelerate growth.
- Voluntary payments reduce the reverse mortgage loan balance to zero over 10 years, with each payment contributing to the growing line of credit.

Financial Illustration:

Age	Line of Credit	Loan Balance	Home Value	Equity
65	$66,300	$175,500	$650,000	$474,500
70	$229,803	$107,156	$790,824	$683,669
75	$457,306	$11,799	$962,159	$950,360
80	$652,740	$0	$1,170,613	$1,170,613
85	$908,249	$0	$1,424,230	$1,424,230
90	$1,263,774	$0	$1,732,794	$1,732,794
95	$1,758,465	$0	$2,108,208	$2,108,208

Assumes 6.18% Expected Interest Rate and 4% Home Value Appreciation

The option to make voluntary reverse mortgage payments introduces a new level of financial freedom for retirees. By exercising this choice, homeowners can accelerate equity growth and build a robust reserve of assets while enjoying greater control over their financial destiny.

This strategic approach not only enhances retirement security, but also fosters peace of mind, allowing individuals to embark on their golden years with confidence and assurance.

Questions: If you had a choice, would you rather your monthly loan payments be mandatory or voluntary? If turning your mortgage payments voluntary meant you could retire on time having given your money 10 more years to grow and create a reserve bucket of assets of nearly $500,000, what would that mean for you?

www.HousingWealthConversations.com/VoluntaryPayments

CONVERSATION #3

PURCHASING A HOME WITH A REVERSE MORTGAGE | THE HIDDEN GEM

Question: If moving to your next, last, and best home meant you could increase your cash flow, reduce your expenses, and add new dollars back to your retirement savings, would you want to see how it works?

Retirement often prompts individuals to consider "rightsizing" their living situation to match their evolving needs and desires. Beyond mere downsizing, rightsizing involves finding a home perfectly suited to one's retirement lifestyle; whether it's closer to family, easier to maintain, or offers amenities for an active life.

Empowering this transition is the reverse mortgage for purchase (HECM for Purchase: H4P), a unique financial tool that enables individuals aged 62 and older to blend a downpayment with loan proceeds from a reverse mortgage. This approach eliminates the need for monthly mortgage payments, offering retirees financial flexibility while preserving savings for other retirement expenses.

Utilizing a reverse mortgage for purchase not only provides financial benefits, but also grants retirees the freedom to select a home that enhances their retirement lifestyle without the burden of monthly mortgage payments. This newfound flexibility allows retirees to allocate income towards enriching their retirement experience.

CLIENT PROFILE

- 65-year-old Archie and Edith are nearing retirement
- Total retirement savings in qualified plans: $250,000
- Current home valued at $750,000 with a $100,000 mortgage | Monthly principal and interest payments: $1,000

CONCERNS, RISKS, GAPS, AND OPPORTUNITIES

Archie and Edith worry that financial constraints may compromise their envisioned retirement lifestyle. They seek a balance between responsible financial planning and personal happiness. The advisor is concerned about potential overspending in the early retirement years compounded by sequence risk, market volatility, and unforeseen expenses eroding their nest egg.

Question: If eliminating monthly mortgage payments could enhance your early retirement experience without financial guilt, what significance would that hold for you?

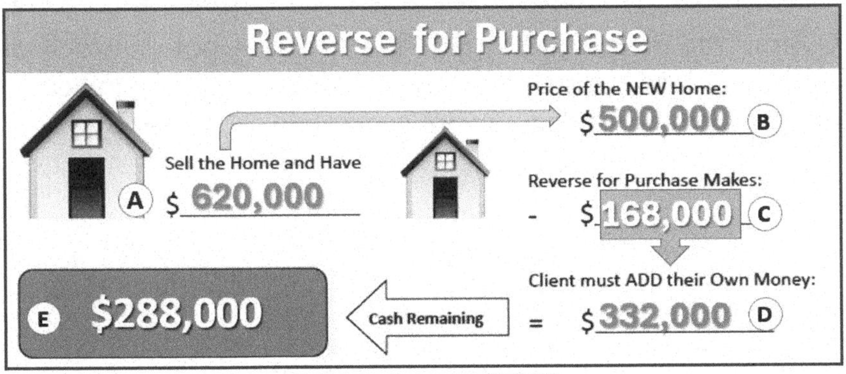

For Illustration Purposes Only | EIR 5.98%

HOW DOES IT WORK?

Utilizing the Reverse Mortgage for Purchase allowed the client to strategically leverage their home sale proceeds to enhance their retirement lifestyle and financial position:

A. With $620,000 from the sale of their previous home,
B. They purchased a $500,000 home, opting not to pay cash up front.
C. The reverse mortgage provided approximately $168,000 in proceeds.
D. The client provided a downpayment of $332,000 completing the retirement home purchase.
E. This left them with $288,000 to bolster their retirement savings without the burden of ongoing mortgage payments.

AS A RESULT:

- Archie and Edith upgraded to a home with newer amenities, lower taxes, and reduced maintenance.
- Their retirement savings increased from $250,000 to $538,000.
- They also gained an additional $1,000 per month in income by eliminating their previous mortgage payments.

Overall, the Reverse Mortgage for Purchase not only facilitated a seamless transition to a new home but also significantly improved the client's financial outlook in retirement.

www.HousingWealthConversations.com/Purchase

CONVERSATION #4

ROTH IRA CONVERSIONS AS A TAX MITIGATION STRATEGY

Question: If you could use your home to reduce the income taxes you pay in retirement, would you want to see how it works?

"When is a million dollars not a million dollars?" goes the riddle. The answer: When those dollars are in a pre-tax IRA or 401(k). In these retirement accounts, the government's share takes precedence, leaving retirees uncertain about their eventual tax obligations.

This uncertainty clouds retirement income planning, particularly as many anticipate rising taxes amid escalating national debt and unfunded liabilities. In this chapter, we delve into mitigating taxes with Roth conversions, preparing for the inevitable financial landscape.

Building upon the foundation of the HECM line of credit, we explore how reverse mortgages offer a tax-efficient solution. As a loan, the proceeds from a reverse mortgage are not subject to income tax, ensuring they do not impact your taxable income. Over the next few chapters, we'll examine specific cases, all anchored in this foundational strategy.

CLIENT SUMMARY

Both aged 65, preparing for retirement, and holding $1,000,000 in IRA/401k accounts, our clients Mickey and

Minnie also own a home valued at $650,000 with no mortgage. They aim to move taxable dollars into non-taxed funds via a Roth conversion but are not sure where to obtain the funds to pay income taxes on the conversion?

Should they use the IRA/401k to pay the income taxes that would be due, or should they take it from some other asset?

ADVISOR CHALLENGE:

The advisor faces the task of structuring a tax-efficient strategy for our clients' retirement funds. Given their goal of Roth conversions, the challenge lies in determining the most optimal source for covering income taxes on the conversions. Should the advisor recommend utilizing assets from the IRA/401k or other assets?

The advisor first suggests that instead of rolling over 100% the funds in the first year, they roll it over $100,000 per year for 10 years. Additionally, he invites them to explore the benefits of leveraging a growing reverse mortgage line of credit to cover the income taxes due on the rollover each year.

REVERSE MORTGAGE MODELING

Age	ReLOC	Growth	Withdrawal for Taxes	Ending ReLOC Balance
65	$206,400	$13,106	($22,000)	$197,506
66	$197,506	$12,541	($22,000)	$188,048
67	$188,048	$11,941	($22,000)	$177,989
68	$177,989	$11,302	($22,000)	$167,291
69	$167,291	$10,623	($22,000)	$155,914
70	$155,914	$9,900	($22,000)	$143,814
71	$143,814	$9,132	($22,000)	$130,947
72	$130,947	$8,315	($22,000)	$117,262
73	$117,262	$7,446	($22,000)	$102,708
74	$102,708	$6,521	($22,000)	$87,230

Mickey and Minnie begin by securing a growing reverse mortgage line of credit (ReLOC), initially accessing $206,400 in available credit.

As the ReLOC matures, it generates a noteworthy $13,106 in growth during the inaugural year.

With their financial plan in motion, the clients embark on a Roth rollover, withdrawing $100,000 from their pre-tax IRAs and 401(k)s. However, this action incurs a tax liability of $22,000. To address this tax obligation, the clients leverage their Reverse Mortgage line of credit to cover the taxes owed.

This strategic approach proves effective, leading the clients to repeat the process over the next nine years until the entirety of their $1 million is successfully converted into Roth accounts. Minnie is thrilled with the amount of hair bows she can now buy.

While this strategy necessitates immediate tax expenditures, the clients recognize the long-term advantages of moving money into Roth IRAs, where there are no RMDs and possible tax-free investment gains. Despite relinquishing the potential growth if the funds were invested conventionally, the utilization of Roth conversions and the ReLOC ensures a tax-efficient approach tailored to their retirement objectives.

The utilization of a reverse mortgage line of credit serves as a pivotal asset in our clients' tax mitigation strategy. By tapping into the ReLOC to cover taxes incurred during Roth conversions, our clients maintain financial flexibility and enhance their retirement planning.

www.HousingWealthConversations.com/Roth

CONVERSATION #5

REDUCING TAXABLE INCOME WITHOUT REDUCING LIFESTYLE

Question: Would you consider limiting your retirement income to your required minimum distributions and supplementing the rest from your home if it could lower that taxes you pay?

In retirement, managing income taxes often means controlling taxable income. By supplementing taxable income with non-taxable sources, you can significantly reduce your tax burden without sacrificing your lifestyle. While Required Minimum Distributions (RMDs) are sometimes unavoidable, minimizing additional withdrawals can be beneficial.

CLIENT SUMMARY AND HECM ASSESSMENT

Our clients June and Ward, set to begin RMDs at age 73, aim to navigate retirement income while minimizing taxes. With a HECM line of credit established today, projected to exceed $300,000 by age 73, they could potentially receive around $2,200 per month through a Tenure Payment option, which would provide equal monthly payments that would be available as long as at least one borrower lives and continues to occupy the property as a principal residence. While it's uncertain if this income will meet their needs beyond RMDs, it's a conversation worth exploring for tax-efficient retirement planning.

Age	LOC Amount	Tenure Payment	5 Year Term	10 Year Term
65	$199,200	$1,221	$3,893	$2,268
70	$277,175	$1,775	$5,416	$3,155
75	$385,672	$2,633	$7,537	$4,390
80	$536,639	$4,036	$10,487	$6,109
85	$746,701	$6,542	$14,592	$8,500
90	$1,038,990	$11,827	$20,304	
95	$1,445,692	$28,251		

$600,000 House Expected Interest Rate: 6.18%

CONVERSATION #6

NAVIGATING SOCIAL SECURITY IN RETIREMENT

Question: Would you be interested in exploring how leveraging your home could provide you with additional Social Security options and mitigate the risk of it being taxed?

Since its inception in 1935, Social Security has been a cornerstone of retirement income for many Americans. Originally designed to cover 35% of a person's total income during a shorter life expectancy, it now constitutes 50% or more of retirement income for most individuals, stretching over a longer lifespan.

CLIENT PROFILE:

Meet our 65-year-old client, Ross. His wife, Rachel, is preparing to retire. Despite Ross being the primary earner and still able to work, recent health concerns cast uncertainty on his life expectancy. Their primary concern revolves around the optimal timing for claiming Social Security benefits and planning for the unexpected. Their advisor shares their apprehensions.

REVERESE MORTGAGE LINE OF CREDIT

Age	LOC Amount	Tenure Payment	5 Year Term	10 Year Term
65	$199,200	$1,221	$3,893	$2,268
70	$277,175	$1,775	$5,416	$3,155
75	$385,672	$2,633	$7,537	$4,390
80	$536,639	$4,036	$10,487	$6,109
85	$746,701	$6,542	$14,592	$8,500
90	$1,038,990	$11,827	$20,304	
95	$1,445,692	$28,251		

$600,000 House Expected Interest Rate: 6.18%

Five Conversations

- **Supplementing Social Security:** Reverse mortgages can bridge the gap between Social Security benefits and retirees' financial needs, enriching their retirement lifestyle.
- **Bridging the Income Gap:** Delaying Social Security until age 70 maximizes benefits, but few wait beyond 66. A 5-year term HECM can provide nearly $50,000 annually, tax-free, until Social Security benefits commence at 70.
- **Avoiding the "Tax Torpedo":** Premature IRA withdrawals can trigger higher taxes on Social Security benefits. Using a HECM line of credit minimizes taxable income, preserving retirement assets and minimizing tax liabilities.
- **Spousal Support:** A reverse mortgage can cushion the financial impact of a spouse's passing, ensuring the surviving partner can maintain their lifestyle.
- **Managing Medicare:** Higher-income retirees may be subject to Income-Related Monthly Adjustment Amount (IRMAA) premiums for Part B (medical care) and Part D (prescription drugs). Leveraging a reverse mortgage to lower taxable income can reduce or eliminate these surcharges, providing significant healthcare cost savings.

By integrating reverse mortgages into their retirement strategy, individuals can navigate Social Security challenges and healthcare expenses with confidence. These strategic conversations empower retirees to optimize their benefits, minimize taxation, and safeguard their financial well-being throughout retirement.

www.HousingWealthConversations.com/SocialSecurity

CONVERSATION #7

ENHANCING ANNUITIES WITH FLEXIBLE LIQUIDITY SOLUTIONS

Question: If we could use your house to replenish the dollars used in creating a fixed income plan, would that be helpful to you?

In the realm of retirement planning, integrating annuities offers a pathway to stability and protection against premature erosion of savings.

These financial instruments, commonly known for their guaranteed payouts, serve as a cornerstone for many retirees seeking financial security. Yet, the challenge arises when clients desire the stability and growth potential of annuities - but hesitate due to the restricted access to their funds.

This chapter explores how the strategic use of reverse mortgages can address this dilemma by providing liquidity, thereby enhancing the conversation around annuities for both advisors and clients alike.

CLIENT PROFILE

Kermit and Miss Piggy, aged 65, currently hold $600,000 in the market. While they seek to hedge against inflation by keeping some assets in the market, they are wary of overexposure. Their goal is to establish a diversified plan by allocating half of their nest egg to fixed income, ensuring coverage for daily expenses while retaining the remaining portion for discretionary spending. Their primary concern revolves around potential liquidity needs exceeding penalty-free withdrawal limits.

Age	LOC Amount	Tenure Payment	5 Year Term	10 Year Term
65	$199,200	$1,221	$3,893	$2,268
70	$277,175	$1,775	$5,416	$3,155
75	$385,672	$2,633	$7,537	$4,390
80	$536,639	$4,036	$10,487	$6,109
85	$746,701	$6,542	$14,592	$8,500
90	$1,038,990	$11,827	$20,304	
95	$1,445,692	$28,251		

$600,000 House Expected Interest Rate: 6.18%

REVERSE MORTGAGE CONVERSATION

I think you are beginning to see a pattern here. With an established line of credit of $199,000, Kermit and Miss Piggy gain immediate and accessible liquidity, coupled with the added benefit of the line of credit growing between 6-8%. This effectively addresses their liquidity concerns.

Additional Question: How beneficial would it be for you if we could utilize your house to replenish the funds utilized in establishing a fixed income plan?

CONVERSATION #8

INTEGRATING LIFE INSURANCE WITH REVERSE MORTGAGES

Question: How beneficial would it be for you if we could utilize your home to replenish the income you are using to pay insurance premiums?

Life insurance stands as a cornerstone of many financial plans, offering both death benefits and valuable life benefits. However, one of the challenges advisors face is ensuring client comfort with premium amounts, particularly in times of economic uncertainty like the Covid-19 pandemic.

CLIENT PROFILE:

Meet Pierce and Linda, aged 65 and retired. They possess a large enough nest egg to weather economic storms but seek life insurance for its tax-free transfer of assets and death benefit, especially considering the husband predeceasing the wife. With a $700,000 home and a $125,000 mortgage, their current monthly mortgage payment is $1,300. After a medical review, their advisor estimates monthly insurance premiums at $2,000.

Though Pierce and Linda can afford these premiums from their income and assets, they remain cautious amid global and economic uncertainty. In navigating this challenge, the advisor presents a third option: leveraging their home equity to replenish the income used for premiums.

REVERSE MORTGAGE SUMMARY

Utilizing a reverse mortgage, Pierce and Linda can eliminate their existing $125,000 mortgage and establish a growing line of credit of $108,400. This effectively frees up $1,300 per month, which in essence is like reducing their life insurance premiums by 2/3.

How does this change the conversation?

By integrating reverse mortgages to replenish income for life insurance premiums, clients like Pierce and Linda can benefit from insurance coverage without financial strain. This innovative strategy ensures asset protection and streamlines wealth transfer to their heirs. As advisors explore novel solutions, the fusion of life insurance and reverse mortgages opens up fresh avenues for client prosperity and long-term financial security.

Age	LOC Amount	Tenure Payment	5 yr Term	10 yr Term
65	$108,400	$665	$2,118	$1,234
70	$150,832	$966	$2,948	$1,717
75	$209,874	$1,433	$4,101	$2,389
80	$292,027	$2,196	$5,707	$3,324
85	$406,337	$3,560	$7,941	$4,625
90	$565,394	$6,436	$11,049	
95	$786,712	$15,374		

www.HousingWealthConversations.com/LifeInsurance

CONVERSATION #9

LONG TERM CARE PLANNING | THE SILENT THREAT IN RETIREMENT

Question: If your home could serve as the foundation of a long-term care plan, safeguarding your other assets from depletion, would you be interested in learning more about how it operates?

Imagine a scenario where your client's home could serve as a cornerstone in their long-term care plan, offering protection for their assets and peace of mind for their future.

This chapter delves into the critical yet often overlooked aspect of long-term care planning and explores how leveraging home equity can help mitigate the financial challenges associated with healthcare and long-term care expenses.

Healthcare and long-term care costs represent significant financial burdens for retirees, with expenses often exceeding expectations. According to a recent Fidelity study, the average 65-year-old couple can expect to incur over $300,000 in healthcare-related expenses during retirement, excluding the costs of long-term care services. These additional expenses can further strain retirement savings, making proactive planning essential.

CLIENT PROFILE:

Meet our 65-year-old clients Mike and Carol, who are both on the brink of retirement. They have diligently saved $450,000 in qualified plans and own a home valued at $600,000. As they prepare for this new chapter in their lives, they face the looming question of how to address potential long-term care needs without depleting their hard-earned assets.

REVERSE MORTGAGE HIGHLIGHTS:

With the utilization of a reverse mortgage, a line of credit of $199,200 becomes available. This pivotal step opens the door to a multitude of discussions and strategies aimed at safeguarding their financial well-being in the face of future healthcare expenses.

Age	Growth	Tenure Pmt	5-yr Term
65	$206,400	$1,219	$4,003
70	$283,645	$1,756	$5,501
75	$389,798	$2,582	$7,559
80	$535,679	$2,769	$10,339
85	$736,155	$6,319	$14,277
90	$1,011,071	$11,350	$19,619
95	$1,390,271	$26,962	

Conversation Guide:

Navigating the complexities of long-term care planning can be daunting, but with the right approach, it becomes a manageable endeavor. Consider these tailored conversation starters:

Daily Costs of Care: Have you considered the benefits of having a financial reserve to cover escalating healthcare expenses? This could include higher deductibles, copayments, prescription costs, and other unforeseen medical emergencies.

Self-Insurance: How would you feel about establishing a reserve fund with the potential to reach $500,000 or more, providing you with accessible funds for any future care needs?

Co-Insurance: While you may already have a long-term care (LTC) policy in place to cover some care costs, would you be interested in exploring additional financial resources as a safety net in case your existing coverage falls short?

Policy Architecture: What if we could adjust certain aspects of your LTC insurance policy, such as extending waiting periods or modifying benefit amounts, to make it more affordable? The flexibility of the reverse mortgage line of credit allows for such adjustments, potentially enhancing the viability of your coverage.

Premium Replenishment: Imagine being able to use your home equity to replenish the funds you allocate towards LTC insurance premiums, providing you with greater peace of mind without directly impacting your day-to-day finances. This strategic use of resources ensures financial stability while addressing your long-term care needs.

By engaging in these conversations and exploring innovative solutions, our clients can proactively plan for their long-term care needs while preserving their financial security and peace of mind.

www.HousingWealthConversations.com/LongTermCare

CONVERSATION #10

COMBINING REVERSE MORTGAGES WITH PORTFOLIO MANAGEMENT | MAXIMIZING RETIREMENT SPENDING

Question: If we could use your home to increase your current spending without risking your nest egg, what would that mean to you?

Imagine a scenario where you could boost your retirement spending without jeopardizing your nest egg. This tantalizing prospect is within reach, thanks to the strategic integration of reverse mortgages and investment portfolios. But how does this synergy work, and what are the benefits for retirees? Let's delve into the details.

In the realm of retirement income planning, the adage "an ounce of prevention is worth a pound of cure" rings true, especially when it comes to starting early. Consider the profound impact of beginning to save at a young age versus delaying until later in life. Small adjustments made early on can yield substantial benefits down the road.

CLIENT PROFILE:

Meet George and Louise, a couple embarking on retirement with $1 million in savings. Their goal is to maintain their lifestyle for the next 33 years. While their advisor recommends an initial withdrawal rate of $39,500 per year, George and

Louise yearn for more flexibility in their spending without risking the longevity of their nest egg.

REVERSE MORTGAGE STRATEGY:

Enter the reverse mortgage line of credit. By leveraging their age, property value, and prevailing interest rates, the HECM offers them a growing line of credit of around $206,000. This financial resource opens new possibilities for enhancing their retirement income.

SIMULATION RESULTS:

Drawing from the research of Dr. Wade Pfau, we examine the impact of different withdrawal strategies on portfolio longevity. Pfau's findings reveal that modest adjustments in annual withdrawals can yield significant long-term benefits. By reducing their withdrawal by as little as $2,000 or $4,000 per year, George and Louise could potentially preserve or even grow their retirement savings over three decades. (See letter B and C on illustration)

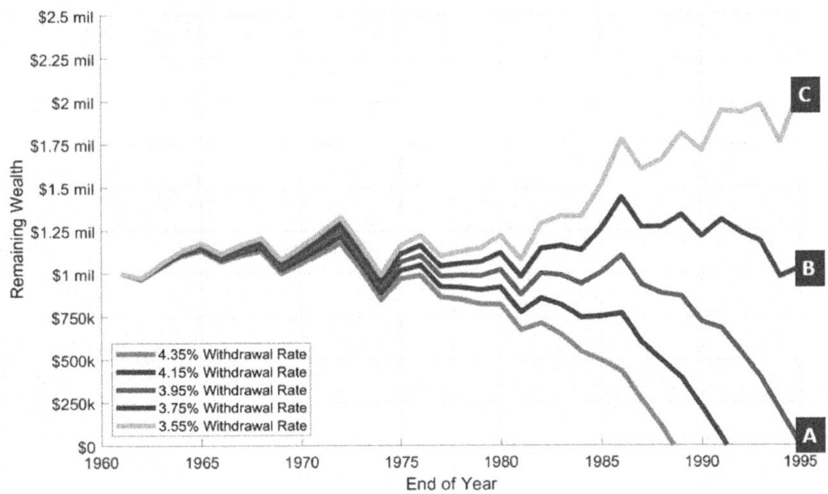

However, George and Louise's primary concern was how they could spend MORE during the early years of their retirement without compromising their nest egg. This, with the

Reverse Mortgage Line of Credit (ReLOC) emerges as a versatile tool in their financial arsenal.

By adhering to their initial withdrawal strategy and supplementing their retirement enjoyment with the ReLOC, they can strike a balance between meeting their desired spending and safeguarding their retirement assets.

In conclusion, the integration of reverse mortgages and portfolios offers retirees a powerful means of maximizing their retirement spending. Through prudent planning and strategic use of resources like the HECM and ReLOC, individuals like George and Louise can enjoy a more comfortable and financially secure retirement. As you embark on your own retirement journey, consider the potential benefits of incorporating these innovative strategies into your financial plan.

CONVERSATION #11

NAVIGATING MARKET VOLATILITY WITH REVERSE MORTGAGES

Question: If we could use your home as a backup plan for market risk and volatility so that you don't prematurely erode your nest egg, what you want to see how it works?

In the wake of market turbulence, the notion of using home equity as a buffer against financial uncertainties has gained traction among financial planners. Inspired by the groundbreaking research of Salter, Pfeiffer, and Evensky, published in the Journal of Financial Planning, the integration of reverse mortgages with portfolio management has emerged as a compelling strategy to maintain spending stability during downturns.

CLIENT PROFILE:

Meet our clients; a 65-year-old couple with $1 million in savings and a desire for an initial withdrawal of $40,000. With a mortgage-free home valued at $650,000, Jim and Pam stand at the precipice of retirement. However, concerns loom regarding the potential impact of market downturns on their nest egg.

CONCERNS, RISKS, GAPS, AND OPPORTUNITIES:

Jim and Pam worry about sustaining their lifestyle in the face of market volatility, while their advisor is mindful of the risks posed by sequence of returns and unplanned expenditures. Together, they seek solutions to mitigate these challenges and ensure financial security throughout retirement.

REVERSE MORTGAGE COORDINATED STRATEGY:

Drawing insights from leading financial experts, including Dr. Wade Pfau, the strategy of refraining from portfolio withdrawals in the year following a market downturn emerges as a key tactic. By utilizing alternative income sources such as cash equivalents, life insurance, or a reverse mortgage line of credit, clients can protect their portfolios and allow them to rebound effectively and last significantly longer.

ILLUSTRATION AND RESULTS:

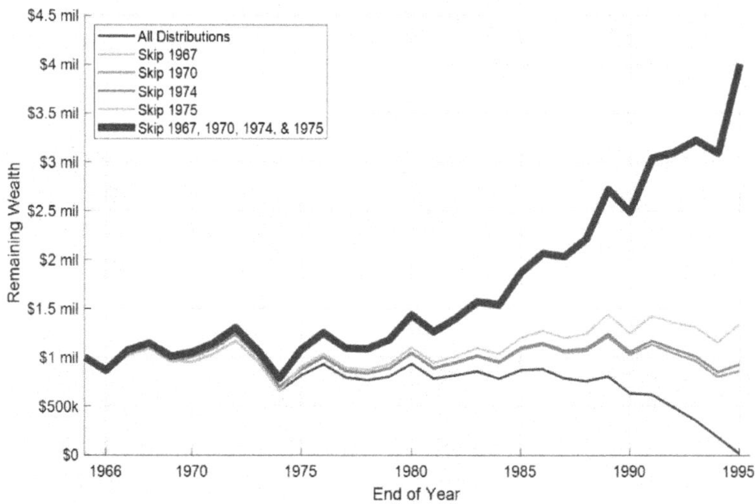

Let's examine the tangible outcomes illustrated in the accompanying chart.

If the client strategically utilizes the reverse mortgage line of credit just once over a 30-year period (choosing the year to skip spending), they could potentially have between $800,000 and $1.2 million assets at the 30-year mark.

However, if they were to leverage the reverse mortgage line of credit **four times** over the same timeframe, particularly in the early years of retirement, the results could be even more striking: a nest egg totaling $4 million compared to potentially zero without this strategic financial tool.

Years	ReLOC Growth	Withdrawal
1	$206,400	$40,000
2	$179,506	$41,500
9	$216,167	$56,000
18	$284,567	$80,000
19	$222,637	$84,000
24	$195,434	$102,000
30	$143,997	$125,000

To underscore the importance of this approach, let's examine a chart that illustrates the establishment of a $206,400 ReLOC.

When the client's investment portfolio faced a downturn, rather than depleting this diminished asset for living expenses, a strategic decision was made to withdraw $40,000 from their line of credit.

In the subsequent year, as the market continued to underperform, an inflation-adjusted sum of $41,500 was drawn from the ReLOC. In subsequent years, inflation-adjusted withdrawals continued.

This method was consistently employed following any market downturns. Rather than drawing from the investment portfolio, funds were accessed from the line of credit. Notably, this strategy was utilized in years 1, 2, 9, 19, 24, and 30, as demonstrated in the table.

Leveraging a reverse mortgage line of credit during financial downturns allows clients to safeguard their retirement assets, thereby fostering the potential for wealth accumulation over the long term. Whether used conservatively or more frequently, the reverse mortgage line of credit serves as a critical component in preserving financial security.

The integration of reverse mortgages with comprehensive portfolio management provides a robust strategy for protecting retirement income and mitigating the effects of market volatility. Through proactive strategies and active management, retirees can confidently navigate their post-career years with enhanced security and financial well-being.

www.HousingWealthConversations.com/VolatilityBuffer

CONVERSATION #12

DISCUSSING REVERSE MORTGAGES WITH HEIRS

In our journey of incorporating reverse mortgages into retirement planning, we've explored the myriad ways in which these financial tools can pave the path to a secure and fulfilling retirement. Yet, as we come to an end, it's essential to address a crucial aspect: How do we help our clients feel at ease when broaching the topic with their heirs?

The Oxygen Mask

In my 25 years of experience, I've found that 99% of children are fine with their parents using their home equity to make their later years better. When I speak with the children, which I regularly do, I often remind them of the last time they flew on an airplane. Do they recall the safety instructions provided by the flight attendants before takeoff, where they say: "In case of an emergency, put your own oxygen mask on first before assisting others"? They usually laugh at this point because they know where the dialogue is going.

This metaphor resonates deeply in the realm of financial planning. Just as individuals must secure their own well-being before aiding others, our clients need to ensure their own financial stability before worrying about the next generation. Picture the reverse mortgage as that financial oxygen mask. By leveraging the equity in their homes through a reverse mortgage, clients can bolster their retirement income, safeguarding their financial future and, by extension, their ability to provide support to their loved ones.

Questions for the Heirs:

1. What are your thoughts or concerns about utilizing home equity through a reverse mortgage? This question opens up the conversation and allows heirs to express any reservations or uncertainties they may have about the concept.
2. What are your primary concerns about inheritance and how the use of a reverse mortgage might impact it? This question encourages heirs to articulate specific worries they may have about their inheritance and how the utilization of home equity could affect it, providing an opportunity for clients to address these concerns directly.
3. How can we honor your parents' wishes and preferences regarding their financial future, including their decision to consider a reverse mortgage?" This question emphasizes the importance of respecting and honoring the autonomy of the parents in making financial decisions that align with their wishes and values, encouraging heirs to support their parents' choices, including the exploration of reverse mortgages, as a means of achieving their desired retirement outcomes.
4. What are some ways you can help alleviate any financial stress or uncertainty your parents may be experiencing in retirement? By acknowledging the potential financial challenges that parents may face in retirement, this question underscores the importance of heirs taking an active role in alleviating their parents' concerns and exploring solutions such as reverse mortgages to enhance their financial stability.
5. What measures can we take to ensure that your parents' financial needs are met, allowing them to age in place comfortably and independently? By shifting the focus to the parents' needs and desires, this question highlights

the importance of supporting their autonomy and well-being, motivating heirs to explore options such as reverse mortgages that facilitate aging in place.

When clients understand that by securing their own financial well-being, they're often better positioned to assist their heirs in the long run, the conversation becomes less daunting.

Back to my Kentucky upbringing: Momma asked me, "Son, when we go, would you rather have the apple tree or the orchard?" I understood. The orchard, of course!

You see, the apple tree represents the house with the equity that remains at the end. The orchard represents the entirety of all the retirement assets, which were preserved but also given opportunities for growth. Moreover, integrating a reverse mortgage into the estate plan doesn't detract from the total inheritance; rather, it can be structured to preserve and even amplify wealth. By leveraging home equity, clients can free up other assets, allowing them to remain invested and potentially grow over time.

In essence, the reverse mortgage serves as a catalyst for expanding the inheritance, enabling clients to pass on a more significant legacy to their loved ones.

Initiating conversations about reverse mortgages with heirs can evoke apprehension and uncertainty. However, by employing metaphors such as the oxygen mask and the apple orchard, we can alleviate these concerns and instill confidence in our clients.

By prioritizing their own financial well-being and adopting a strategic approach to wealth management, clients can pave the way for a brighter future—for themselves and for generations to come.

www.HousingWealthConversations.com/Legacy

CLOSING THOUGHTS

As we close the pages of this journey together, it's essential to reflect on the profound role that empathy and understanding play in the realm of retirement planning, especially when introducing concepts like housing wealth and reverse mortgages to our clients.

This Quick Start Guide has not only equipped you with the technical knowledge and strategic approaches necessary for navigating these conversations but has also underscored the importance of connecting with clients on a human level.

Armed with these skills, you are now better prepared to guide your clients through the full range of their options with both competence and compassion, ensuring that their retirement years are not just secure, but truly enriching.

Remember, the integration of housing wealth into retirement planning isn't just about the numbers; it's about unlocking possibilities, providing peace of mind, and crafting legacies.

Together, we can redefine retirement planning to include the critical, yet often overlooked, component of housing wealth - ensuring a more comprehensive and client-focused advisory practice.

Next Steps for Handling a Client or Case:

- Visit www.HousingWealthPro.com to request a Housing Wealth Illustration, which will provide an estimate of your client's potential benefits from a reverse mortgage.
- Get in touch via email at AskDonGraves@gmail.com
- Set up a consultation at www.AskDonGraves.net
- Alternatively, you can reach us directly by calling 215-732-0814

Made in USA - Kendallville, IN
11597_9781732027053
04.09.2024 1451